Clouds

Look for the other books on weather by

Marion Dane Bauer
Snow • Rain • Wind
Rainbow • Sun

Simon Spotlight
An imprint of Simon & Schuster Children's Publishing Division
1230 Avenue of the Americas, New York, NY 10020
This Simon Spotlight edition May 2016
First Simon Spotlight edition September 2011
First Aladdin edition February 2004
Text copyright © 2004 by Marion Dane Bauer
Illustrations copyright © 2004 by John Wallace
For information about special discounts for bulk purchases, please contact
Simon & Schuster Special Sales at 1-866-506-1949
or business@simonandschuster.com.
Book design by Debra Sfetsios
The text of this book was set in Century Schoolbook.
Manufactured in the United States of America 0222 LAK
20
Library of Congress Cataloging-in-Publication Data
Bauer, Marion Dane.
Clouds / Marion Dane Bauer; illustrated by John Wallace.—1st
p. cm. — (Ready-to-read)
Summary: Illustrations and simple text explain three types of clouds,
stratus, cumulus, and cirrus.
1. Clouds—Juvenile literature. [1. Clouds.] I. Wallace, John, 1966–
ill. II. Title. III. Series.
QC921.35 .B38 2004
551.57'6—dc21
2002009526
ISBN 978-1-4814-6213-6 (hc)
ISBN 978-0-689-85441-5 (pbk)
ISBN 978-1-4424-9951-5 (eBook)

Clouds

written by Marion Dane Bauer

illustrated by John Wallace

Ready-to-Read

Simon Spotlight
New York London Toronto Sydney New Delhi

Can you make a cloud?

Breathe out on a cold day.

See your breath?
You have made a cloud.

Can you walk in a cloud?
Fog is a cloud
stretched along the ground.

Have you ever walked in fog?

There are three kinds
of clouds.
Cirrus.
That means "curl."

Curl clouds are wisps
high in the sky.

Stratus.

That means "layered"
or "spread out."
Fog is a layered cloud.

A layered cloud may cover
your entire state.

Layered clouds can be
thick and gray.

They may bring
rain or snow.

Cumulus.

That means "heap" or "pile."

Heap clouds can grow
tall and dark.
They may bring a thunderstorm!

Clouds are made of
water vapor
or ice crystals.

Clouds keep us cooler
in the day.
They give us shade.

Clouds keep us warmer
at night.
They make a blanket
to hold Earth's heat in.

Clouds bring us
rain and snow.

They send our water
back to us.

The water in our clouds
once bathed dinosaurs!

Now it bathes us!

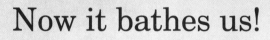

Facts about clouds:

 Water vapor droplets are so small you would need a microscope to see one.

 It would take seven billion water vapor droplets to make one tablespoon of water.

Even a small cloud can be as heavy as ten large elephants.

If a cloud is made of water, you can see its edges.

If a cloud is made of ice, the edges fade into a blue sky.